# You're Invited:

## A Non-Fluffy, Straight-To-The-Point, Easy-To-Digest Perspective On Why Belonging Is Best For Business

Kristen Bakalar

**You're Invited:** *A Non-Fluffy, Straight-To-The-Point, Easy-To-Digest Perspective On Why Belonging Is Best For Business*

Copyright © 2021 by Kristen Bakalar. All rights reserved.

No part of this book may be used or reproduced in any manner whatsoever without written permission from the copyright owner except in the case of brief quotations embodied in larger pieces of work.

To request permission, contact kristen@kristenbakalar.com

The information and sources cited were accurate at the time of publication, but the Author does not assume any liability for loss of damage caused by errors or omission. Because of the dynamic nature of the internet, any web addresses contained in this book may have changed since publication and may no longer be valid.

Copy Editor: Beth Knaus

kristenbakalar.com

# Table of Contents

## INTRODUCTION
    The Premise                                    2
    The Goal of the Invitation                     8
    The Question That Started It All              13

## SECTION 1: ORGANIZATIONAL RELATIONSHIPS
    The Honest Recruiter                          17
    Nondiscrimination Statements                  21
    The Usual Suspects                            25
    Culture Defined                               29

## SECTION 2: INDIVIDUAL RELATIONSHIPS
    Annie                                         36
    Eggshells                                     47

## SECTION 3: TEAM RELATIONSHIPS
    Letting Go                                    59
    Feedback As a Gift                            64
    Any Questions?                                69
    The Perimeter                                 73

## SECTION 4: INVITING DIVERSITY
    Value Connection over Perfection              79

*To my brother Kevin.
Without you, who would I be?*

## ACKNOWLEDGEMENTS

Even though my name is on the cover, I have learned that writing a book is a team sport. And the best thing about the team that helped make this book a reality, is that they are my team even without a special project on the horizon. They are just amazing and supportive members of my personal community, and people who are always willing to help me, support me, and encourage me. They are my challengers, my cheerleaders, my hand-holders, and the people that would *likely* bail me out of jail.

First, I want to thank my partner, Chris Olex. Chris is both the rock that stands strong in contrast to the raging river, and the water that perseveres past the obstacles in her way. She is the best person I know, something I tend to tell her after a cocktail (or three), and there has never been a doubt in my mind about how solidly she stands in my corner.

I need to thank Anita Leto, the inspiration for the book, and a source of unending light at the end of what could be a very dark tunnel. I want to thank Terry Whitaker for her unending support and wisdom that has been constant for decades, and for stepping into this project at a pivotal moment to shift the book in a new direction, entirely. I am appreciative of Amy Goldfarb, for balancing the role of coach, friend, and part-time therapist, and for being the ear, eye, and [sexy] voice that I needed. And a special thanks to Reggie Pearse for offering his expertise and professional advice while aiming his "you go girl" spirit in my direction.

I am grateful for Leah Clark, one of my favorite people with whom to geek out, for her continued partnership and friendship that regularly jumps the fence from professional to personal. I am thankful for Brian Hughes for his willingness and eagerness to brainstorm, and to Scott Mason for his confidence in and continuous support of my potential. Thanks to Cyndi Tarbell, for profoundly boosting my professionalism and not letting me belittle myself, even unintentionally. To Eugene Shim, my gratitude for your business-mindedness, detail-orientation, and eagerness to help knows no bounds; I owe you a bottle of bourbon.

Thank you, Sara Henry, for inspiring me to rethink what I actually think, and thank you Charlotte Dietz for inviting more of my sass and spunk to be experienced by the reader. I'm grateful for Stacie Toal and her no-bullshit approach to feedback that challenged me in all the right ways, and to Greg Olex for offering a perspective from beyond the workplace. And a big thank you goes to the most helpful stranger I've met, Rhonda Morin, for her courage and candor that pushed me to new revelations.

I am indebted to my dear friend Kelly Ceynowa, an early-stage reader, who taught me the valuable and hilarious lesson about the difference between a noun and a verb, and to Laura Cruz for loaning me the unique lens through which she sees the world. A heartfelt thank you goes to Megan Sireci, my work wife, (avid reader that she is) for helping me implement the story structure, finding the spirit of my intention, and helping bring it to life.

Lastly, I am sending my deepest appreciation and admiration to my nieces, who remain beautifully unaware of the countless ways they inspire me. May they both learn the power of the invitation in their own way, in their own time…so their favorite aunt can someday say "I told you so."

*To the subjects (whose names have been changed) - you know who you are. Thank you for inviting me, and for being willing to be written about, even anonymously.*

## INTRODUCTION

*I invite you to be courageous, to dig into your discomfort, and to position curiosity at the core of your success*

## The Premise

This is not a self-help book, nor is it a diversity masterclass, and it's certainly not a replacement for a course in emotional intelligence. This is a book about relationships. It is about building meaningful relationships at work, though let's be honest with each other here: what we learn in life is good for work and what we learn at work is good for life. So while the majority of my examples are about relationships in the workplace, they can all be applied to our personal relationships as well. This book provides a practical approach to strengthening and deepening our relationships while optimizing them for both the company's benefit and for the employees (and people) with whom we share our days. The result: a win-win! The company will realize higher levels of output while the employees will experience higher levels of satisfaction. Let's dive in, shall we?

**The door to meaningful relationships is opened with an invitation.**

This book is for leaders, managers, Human Resources practitioners, and any professional who wants to build and bolster their relationships on the job. We spend over a third of our lives working, and as our professional lives and our personal lives continue to overlap and intertwine, our relationships become more intersectional and more meaningful.

Our friends are our colleagues, our managers are our mentors, our living rooms are our offices, our workplaces are our coffee shops. We talk about work at dinner, and we talk about dinner at work. The lines between the office and the home are being increasingly blurred, making it even more crucial to have quality relationships that fulfill some of the most primal needs we have.

With few exceptions, employees thrive on significant interactions while at work. Whether that is through collaborating on a project, brainstorming new approaches to solve old problems, or enjoying lunch with colleagues, employees' connections with one another are critical to work satisfaction. Susan David, the founder of the Harvard/McLean Institute of Coaching and author of the book *Emotional Agility*, asserts that a lack of connection at work can have a real impact on employees.

> "Without friendships at work, you miss out on two types of important support: structural support which is the 'ability to ask someone to cover for you when you're in a bind,' and emotional support which is having someone to talk you through stress, change, or anxiety," says David.

Beyond friendships at work, having strong relationships with coworkers and leaders also brings a significant benefit to the company. When we have a real connection with our manager, we are more likely to work harder and be more committed. When we have a real connection with our colleagues, we are more likely to give our discretionary effort to the team. When we have quality relationships, we are more likely to find purpose in our work-life. BetterUp Labs, a San Francisco-based leadership development platform, found that "nine out of 10 career professionals would sacrifice 23 percent of their future earnings - an average of $21,000 a year - for 'work that is always meaningful.'" While meaningful work is certainly connected to the company's mission, employees also find meaning in the relationships that exist within the organization.

**Who we work with is just as important as the work we do.**

> BetterUp's research highlighted more benefits to finding meaning at work:
> - Employees who find work meaningful put in an average of one extra hour per week
> - They take fewer days of paid leave
> - They express higher levels of job satisfaction, which links to greater productivity
> - They generate an additional $5,437 per worker per year
> - For every 10,000 managers who view their work as highly meaningful, a company saves $55 million in turnover costs.

In this book, I will share some real stories with real tips for real connection. Sometimes, that connection leads to increased diversity. Sometimes that connection leads to higher levels of inclusion. Sometimes that connection leads to better business outcomes. *Every* time, that connection leads to better and deeper relationships, which are critical ingredients for meaningful work. And when we are engaged in purposeful work *together*, the camaraderie, belongingness, and kinship that emerges is unparalleled, and becomes a differentiator; the differentiator for which companies are searching. The first step to igniting those relationships is simple and profound: an invitation.

**Invitation is the gateway drug to belonging.**

Throughout my career, I have developed an intense pursuit to create more human-centric, inviting organizations. This quest has emerged through formal programming in HR departments, consulting to various organizations on leadership characteristics and company culture, building community in the various places I've lived, and even writing a book like this. And though it is not part of the existing corporate paradigm, where we put profits over people, results over relationships, money over mental health, and stoicism over showing emotion, this *is* what's best for business. A culture of invitation is one that drives results. A culture of invitation helps produce innovative products and creative solutions. A culture of invitation will breed customer loyalty. And as a bonus, it can bridge divides in our communities, it can fuel a deeper connection with each other, and maybe – just maybe – heal some of the wounds of a splintered society. Shifting to an invitation mindset can make an indelible mark on the way we do business and the way we engage with our customers, clients, employees, leaders, stakeholders, and supporters.

In the following pages, I will highlight how a mindset of invitation can strengthen our workplaces, aid in creating a more inclusive culture, and deepen our relationships to each other. I will share some stories that might inspire you to be more invitational, and if you're looking for more of a 'how-to' guide, I invite you to download the companion workbook available at kristenbakalar.com.

I invite you to challenge yourself and the way you approach this topic.
I invite you to be open and willing to ask questions.
Again, I invite you to be courageous, to dig into your discomfort, and to position curiosity at the core of your success.

**Will you accept my invitation?**

## The Goal of the Invitation

To start, think back to middle school. Blech! I know, I know. But all the birthday parties, bar or bat mitzvahs, quinceaneras, and other celebrations, are great examples of the power of an invitation. Consider these simple questions:

**When you got the invitation to your classmate's party, how did you feel?**

There was probably some excitement. You likely felt seen. The invitation probably signaled that you belonged. Maybe there was even some anticipation about who else would be there, what you might wear, what you should bring, what sort of gift you could buy. And it's likely that you felt a sense of confidence, knowing that someone wanted you to join them in their celebration. Kimmy Graco invited me to her sleepover party in fifth grade, even though I wasn't part of her inner clique of friends. I felt like the coolest kid there. (Looking back, I'm pretty sure I *was* the coolest kid there).

**When you did *not* get the invitation, how did you feel?**

Left out? Excluded? Sad? Self-conscious? Ashamed? Maybe you felt like you were not good enough, cool enough, smart enough, or popular enough. It's possible that you thought of things you should have changed about yourself in order to get invited. I distinctly remember sixth grade, when Donny DeLuca had a birthday party and everyone on our baseball team was invited, except for me. Being the only girl on the team, my parents could easily rationalize why I wasn't invited, but none of the explanations made any difference: I was devastated. *"If only I was a boy..."* I thought. And that is the common explanation for those of us who didn't get invited: *if only I was someone else*. We internalize that rejection and it severely impacts our self-worth.

If you can recall the painful experience of being excluded, you are not alone. Not getting the invitation to the party is a primal example of being excluded, and those memories are carved in our brains forever. In fact, many studies found that when people are excluded, the part of their brain that gets stimulated is the same part that is activated by physical pain[1]. The brain can't tell the difference between physical pain, and the feeling of rejection, so when we don't get invited to key meetings or when our ideas are ignored, the pain we feel is real. It is experienced in the same areas of the brain as physical pain.

**Based on that science, the old saying that *"sticks and stones will break my bones but names will***

---

[1] https://kids.frontiersin.org/article/10.3389/frym.2017.00046

***never hurt me"* is now, scientifically speaking of course, bullshit.**

In addition, researchers Roy Baumeister and Mark Leary found that when people are excluded, their intellectual performance drops, as well[2]. Specifically impacted is "logical reasoning, in making links between information, and in the ability to make inferences or draw conclusions from information." These skills are exactly the kind of intellectual processes we rely on in the workplace. We need our employees to connect concepts, translate information into decisions, and use logic to drive business results. So, excluding folks - even unintentionally - is bad for business.

The flip side, however, is getting the invitation to the party and feeling included and ready to participate. Studies cited in Psychology Today show that a sense of belonging has been connected to increased performance, higher levels of motivation, increased happiness, lower levels of stress, and lower instances of depression[3]. In fact, the brain's reward system responded similarly to social recognition as it did to money! So, there are tangible benefits to creating meaningful relationships where every employee feels that they belong.

---

[2] https://headheartbrain.com/resources/how-an-understanding-of-neuroscience-can-help-create-inclusion/
[3] https://www.psychologytoday.com/us/blog/between-cultures/201704/belonging

By *inviting* people in, we are taking the guesswork out of whether or not they belong. We're *telling* them in an explicit, proactive way. This invitation minimizes the negative impact of exclusion. Instead, it connects people to each other, brings teams closer, and strengthens organizations. When employees feel included, excited, and ready to participate, they are more committed to the organization and the company is the beneficiary of their best efforts. Our responsibility in fostering that inclusion, excitement, and participation lies in our ability to invite others to the proverbial party.

## Invite

[ *verb* in-**vahyt**; *noun* **in**-vahyt ]

*To request the presence or participation of in a kindly, courteous, or complimentary way...*

As evidenced by the definition above, the word "invite" is a verb, and if my grammar lessons from first grade taught me anything, that means it's an action word. It requires us to *DO something*. This is the most crucial element of invitation as a mindset: it is rooted in action. It is not a spectator sport. To invite someone to a party, or Thanksgiving dinner, or a meeting, or a conversation requires proactive outreach, and explicit action. Remember the movie *Forrest Gump*? When Forrest got on the bus and one by one people said *"seat taken"* they were clearly being exclusive.  When he got to Jenny, she didn't just say nothing - she **invited** Forrest to sit (in the sweetest voice he had ever heard).  And so he did.  That was a pure example of an invitation.  Had she said nothing, it's unclear whether Forrest would have sat with her or not, but what is certain: her invitation was a proactive outreach, met with action, and he automatically felt included.

Of course, any person who receives an invitation can reject or refuse it.  They have options.  Forrest could have politely declined Jenny's invitation to sit, and the person you invite to Thanksgiving can simply say "no."  But typically, when people get invited, they are more likely to engage.  Typically, when people feel invited to participate, it creates a sense of belonging.  At work, this belongingness translates into better ideas, higher levels of innovation, increased market share, and solutions that are far superior to that which the problem requires.  In the simplest of terms: it makes it so employees want to get out of bed to come to work!

## The Question That Started It All

Years ago, at a local HR event aimed at disrupting the status quo, I stood on the stage with the warm lights beaming down on me. The audience peered playfully at me, their eyes joyfully jumping between the images on the screen and my animated presentation, eager to see and hear what came next. They laughed at my jokes, they nodded along with my stories, and they didn't hold it against me when a slide mysteriously went missing. The nervousness I felt in my chest just moments prior dissipated as I continued hearing the sounds of enjoyment echo amongst the crowd. And then I asked a question that unleashed a fury of excitement and intrigue: *"What if the I in D&I stood for invitation?"*

> "D&I" is a moniker for "diversity and inclusion," two words that - at the time - were at risk of becoming corporate jargon but had yet to become commonplace. In the corporate world, many, if not most organizations are trying to increase the diversity of their employees and ensure that all workers feel included in the workplace. Hence the terms "diversity and inclusion," which is currently a full-blown, prospering industry in and of itself.

I finished the talk, took a mere moment to appreciate the applause, and left the stage, making room for the next speaker of the event. Having no friends or colleagues in the audience to speak with directly (no pity necessary here), I did what I thought best: I went to the bar. With a drink now safely in my hand, I directed my attention to the stage from which I had just come. But little did I know, a small line of people was forming, filled with curious minds that wanted to talk with me, to engage deeper with the concept of D&I, and to explore how "invitation" could become part of their daily lives.

When the evening ended, I wrapped up my conversations, and quietly made my way home. Entering my apartment, I opened the door, took off my shoes, removed my jacket, took a long sigh, and made myself a(nother) cocktail. As I sipped on my Manhattan, I allowed each sip of bourbon to slowly bring me back to the reality I knew. I reflected on the evening and thought more deeply about why "invitation" felt so revolutionary for some when it felt somewhat ordinary to me. I realized that though I had developed the presentation in the weeks leading up to that evening, the need for invitation had been crystallized years before, and it wasn't just about D&I.

The need for invitation cuts through almost every slice of life - we have all "not been invited" at one time or another. From romantic relationships to mentorships to networking to innovation to mother-daughter relationships to manager-employee relationships, and more, it is human nature to want to be invited. It is psychologically predictable and behaviorally validated.

**Let's explore, shall we?**

# SECTION 1:
# ORGANIZATIONAL RELATIONSHIPS

## The Honest Recruiter

**The story:**

Realizing my growth potential was limited where I was, I began a job search and was patiently waiting for the right opportunity to emerge. What a privilege it was to be patient and not just take the first job offer that came my way! And with that privilege of time and financial security, I was able to weigh options, consider choices, and explore alternatives. For the first time in my life, I was able to run *towards* something great, rather than *away* from something...well...not-so-great. So the search went on. And I interacted with several recruiters whose main goal was to put "butts in seats," an HR-ish term that implies a quantity- and numbers-based approach to hiring. Companies who deploy a "butts in seats" approach to recruiting are typically focused on just filling vacancies, rather than finding the best talent for the roles. In other words, those recruiters are really just sales people disguised as members of a Human Resources function.

Several companies take a different approach, and I'm particularly beholden to one company specifically for the invitation I received. Instead of being 'tough' negotiators, pitting one candidate against another, and using forceful sales tactics, they offered an honest and vulnerable invitation.

*"Bottom line, Kristen: we really want you to come work with us."*

And with that, I accepted the job offer, rejecting my other options. This wasn't a sales ploy, a conquest, or a feat. They weren't trying to get the best deal, they weren't playing hard-to-get. They wanted me, and they told me they wanted me. And you know what? *I wanted to be wanted.*

Their invitation to me was clear. And as a result, I trusted their intentions, and I reciprocated with their same level of vulnerability and honesty. The company fed into my emotional desires for connection, they tickled my inner need to be included, and in doing so, they hired an employee who was committed and eager to contribute. I started my employment with the company looking for ways to exceed their expectations. By simply being truthful and sharing that they wanted me to join the company (both incredibly simple actions), they got the best version of me. They got my discretionary effort. They got my best ideas, my best intentions, and my best self.

In turn, I was more confident. I felt good about myself, and I felt safe knowing that I was desired. I wasn't the candidate who they could get cheapest or fastest; I was the candidate that they wanted. Period.

*Simple actions yield profound results.*

**Out with the old:** play hardball with the candidate to get the best "value," or play it cool with the candidate to show you have more options. In other words, put the candidate on the defensive and give them reason to question your integrity as an employer.

**In with the new:** be honest with the candidate, and tell them that you want them to join your company so they feel committed and engaged from the beginning

**What else:** Take more time in the interview process, get to know your candidates personally and professionally. When you decide on the person you want, tell them. In no uncertain terms, tell them you want them. Then tell them why, tell them how you see them contributing, what problems they can help solve, and what challenges they might face in your organization. Be honest and vulnerable. Build trust, be authentic, and tell the truth. By "selling" them on the opportunity, you may cloud your judgment on who the best candidate will be. You or the candidate might make a bad decision. But by being honest about the position and all it entails, and inviting the person to be part of it, you're helping to ensure that the new hire is committed to the organization, even with all its warts. The U.S. Department of Labor estimates the cost of a bad hire at upward of 30% of their first-year salary. That can get costly. Mitigate that risk up front by bringing more candor and vulnerability into the hiring process.

## Nondiscrimination Statements

**The Story:**
During the same job search as referenced earlier, I took particular interest in the nondiscrimination statements on job descriptions. To be fair, statements like these were probably present in all of my prior job searches, but I didn't pay as close attention until more recently. Most of these statements were small, and hidden in the footer of the document, next to the page number, and perhaps near the company name or logo. They tended to read something like this:

> *"We do not and shall not discriminate on the basis of race, color, religion, gender, gender expression, age, national origin, disability, marital status, sexual orientation, or military status, in any of our activities or operations."*

I'd say this type of statement is "standard." It's legal. But it's not enough.

It's likely that most of us have felt marginalized in some way at some point in our lives. But as a proud member of the LGBTQ community, a group of people who have historically been discriminated against, there is nothing about the above statement that makes me feel safe, open, or excited to apply to this company. This statement - the typical language on most job descriptions - reads as an obligatory statement devoid of any authenticity or spirit. I don't trust it. Quite frankly, it scares me. The company has basically said "we will do the bare minimum and only that which is required by law..." It's like they are doing it because someone said they have to. And the intention is only to protect the company from legal retaliation, not to make the individuals in their company feel safe and protected. It protects the company while *stating* that it protects me. Eyeroll.

Given the rising number of employees who are not necessarily in a "protected" class (those who are protected by law from employment discrimination based on race, color, national origin, sex, religion, age, disability, and genetic information), but who care deeply about issues of diversity, equity, inclusion, intersectionality, safety, and the like, this statement not only deters *them* but the very people they want to see hired. Companies that default to the standard will only attract employees who feel safe with the status quo, and those of us pushing for change will go elsewhere.

If we are serious about wanting to increase and improve the diversity and inclusion of our company, we need to do better.

> *"We value and work to leverage the diversity we have in our company and know that a more diverse, inclusive and human culture will improve our*

*business results, and the communities in which we live and work. As such, we invite people of all races, colors, religions, genders, gender expressions, ages, national origins, abilities, sexual orientations, and military experiences to apply to our open positions."*

With this statement, it is clear that the company has put a stake in the ground in identifying a business case for more diversity, and has created an invitation to apply to their positions. The message I hear is that my differences would be *valued*. Because of this statement, I believe that this company wants me to apply, that they want the diversity I bring, that they want the talent I have, and that I will be safe along the way. I take the legality for granted, and I trust that the company would do anything they could to protect me if something nefarious ever happened.

With the first statement, I don't trust the company; with the second, I do. And without trust, what do we have?

**Out with the old:** leading with what we will NOT do (discriminate) as a company.

**In with the new:** leading with what we WILL do (value inclusion and invite diverse candidates) as a company, what we value, and being explicit about the people we want.

**What else:** Go beyond what is legal. The law is far behind the moral compass of many of us applying to open positions. Update your job descriptions with more inviting language. And while you're at it, update the required documents so they include a lens of invitation. And if you're the type to worry that this approach is somehow limiting to the majority, or somehow reduces the number of opportunities for those of us who are used to getting them…you're wrong. This doesn't close the door for some; it opens the door for all. So, don't let the legal threshold dictate your morality statements, and don't be shy in advertising who you want to employ.

## The Usual Suspects

**The Story:**
I was the newly appointed leader of the learning and development department at a medium sized company (~5000 employees). Like many leaders who are new in the role, I talked to dozens of employees and tried to understand their current way of operating as a team and in the company. The modus operandi at the time was to publish training courses and opportunities on our internal Learning Management System (LMS). Then, employees could go through the company's intranet, find the learning portal, search for upcoming classes, and sign up. After the course, the LMS would automatically send them an evaluation and they could then rate the effectiveness of the course.

This is an approach that many companies use to offer learning opportunities to their employees. As a bonus, they likely get some data for how many people attend courses, which courses are most popular, and the people who are signing up for development opportunities. What we found at my previous company, however, is that with such a passive approach to learning and development, most of our employees weren't actually learning or being developed. Because the approach required each individual employee to proactively search, find, and request the opportunity to learn, the only employees who were signing up were the thirstiest and most eager to enhance their skills (or possibly those who were just plain bored). That meant that the more complacent, less motivated employees (who are often the ones who need development the most) remained snug in their comfort zone, content with their current level of output and behavior. To be fair, it is often way more enjoyable to have "the thirstiest and most eager" employees in the classroom than the contrary, but it actually poses a bigger threat to the organization.

Having the same people attending the courses equates to a significant amount of money to develop only a small number of people. The effect on the organization was disproportionate to the budget we were spending, and more importantly, the people who most needed the development were not getting it. Therefore, we weren't changing behavior or improving performance across the organization.

So we switched to a method of invitation. We put the invitation first, and left the behind-the-scenes administration of the LMS exactly where it belongs: behind the scenes. We targeted specific cohorts of employees and sent them invitations to attend a relevant training course. We used inviting language like "we want you…" or "you've been identified as someone who could benefit from…" or "you're a bad-ass, and we want to invest in our bad-ass talent…" That language made most of the employees feel valued and important. It made them feel seen. They were more likely to accept our invitation, and more likely to show up eager and ready to contribute.

The number of people who attended the training courses skyrocketed! We also noticed the engagement level in the classroom was palpably higher, too (an unexpected bonus). The quantity and quality of the evaluations increased, and the buzz in the organization started to hum.

The evidence was clear: people want to be invited. And, oftentimes, they *wait* to be invited.

**Out with the old**: put company events, training opportunities, and the like on the intranet and in the various systems and hope people find them and sign up.

**In with the new**: find the people you want to attend your events and proactively invite them.

**What Else**: Target potential learners, invite them to your courses, and tell them why they are the right "fit" for the opportunity. You can even tailor the course to that specific audience to make them feel more welcomed (a simple change in the title can also make a big difference). When an employee receives an invitation that identifies them as special in some way, they immediately feel valued. They feel seen, identified, paid attention to. They feel invested in. They feel like they matter. It's easy to assume that employees just want money, but in reality, they want to feel valued. And when employees feel like they are valued in the organization, and that the company wants to invest in them, they are eager to invest their time and effort back into the company. Again, it's a win-win. According to research conducted by Opportunity Now, employees who feel included are more loyal to their team and organization, more motivated to go the extra mile, and more productive[4]. Even if you are rolling out a mandatory training course for all managers, send the invitation that tells them that they matter, and that you want them in the room. Tell them that the company believes in them and that they are important and valued. This reassurance can make all the difference.

---

[4] http://shapiroconsulting.co.uk/wp-content/uploads/2013/09/Inclusive-Leadership-Executive-Summary.pdf

## Culture Defined

**The Story:**
Culture is hard to define. It can be a bit of a slippery topic, nebulous in nature, and feel soft to many. In reality, culture is the way work gets done; it's not soft at all, but rather the cause of disruption to our business or the reason for its success. I worked for a company that had recently transitioned from public to private through a private equity takeover. The CEO was ousted as part of the process, and subsequently almost the entire executive team had turned over. It was an interesting (read: titillating, excruciating, hard, fun, curious, exciting, dangerous) time to dissect culture.

The new CEO conducted an off-site retreat with his new leadership team and as part of their conversations, they developed new corporate values. They came back from their retreat and announced them to the thousands of employees via an all-employee email. The values, which sounded like they could have been found on page 158 of any corporate management playbook, quickly became a joke amongst an increasingly resentful workforce. The values (often confused for 'culture'), were generic, at best, and hypocritical at worst: how could one value the value that has no value to them? The employee response was a proverbial, and in some cases explicit eye roll, accompanied by a profound dismissal of any need for behavior change. Like the wave making its way through a stadium full of sports fans, the eye roll made its way from one team to the next; a generic response to a generic action. The HR team was then left holding the bag of corporate jargon with the arduous task of embedding new values into the fabric of the organization. This was an uphill battle, and one that could have been avoided with a simple invitation.

Fast forward one year. I left that organization and was hired at a global technology company to help them define their culture. They had recently been acquired, they were growing rapidly, expanding into new geographies, and working hard to keep their identity intact. But there was one problem: they weren't quite sure what their identity was. Similar to the first company, they were in need of a precise definition of their culture to help anchor their workforce. But despite their identity crisis, this company was confident in its culture. They had a moniker for their culture; they called it "EpicGreen," which was a play off the color of their logo and branding. The lore inside the company was that the founder could allegedly look at any employee and know - instinctively - if he or she was truly "EpicGreen." But during my interview process, I asked almost everyone with whom I met what it meant to be "EpicGreen." No one knew. The best answer I got was "it's just a feeling."

Them: *"It's just a feeling"*
Me: *"Ok, what does it feel like?"*
Them: *"Mmm, I don't know, I can just see it in someone."*
Me: *"Ok, what do you see?"*
Them: *"Mmm, I don't know, I can just tell in the way they carry themselves"*
Me: *"Ok, how would you describe how they carry themselves?"*
Them: *"Mmm, I don't know…"*

This went on and on…

There are many problems with this approach: if we (the "universal" we, that is) rely on a gut feeling, or the innate sense of the founder to uphold the corporate culture, we are setting ourselves up for failure. We will inadvertently hire the same type of person over and over again, leading to a very homogenous culture. We will accidentally reward or punish behavior that is inconsistent, and we will hold people to standards of which they are unaware.

I felt a great deal of pressure - and honor - to be responsible for putting words and actions to what had historically been nothing more than a sensation. I needed to give the culture a definition that could be written down, observed, and measured, all without losing the spirit and the essence that made it special. This was also a big undertaking for the company. It was a vulnerable and brave choice for the founders to entrust me with this task, and I did not want to let them down. As a new employee, it would be fairly arrogant (and ineffective) to think that I would know what the culture was, so I invited the employees to tell me what they thought. I went on an international road show. I sent out surveys, I interviewed employees, I analyzed existing data sources, and I got input from the founders. I asked questions, I invited as many voices as I could find, and I listened.

Within 90 days, I had a definition of this company's culture that was not some "pie-in-the-sky" definition, or something that was created in a private boardroom by leaders who were out of touch with the day-to-day happenings of their companies. This definition was created by and for the people. And when it was presented back to them, they were elated. One by one, smiles emerged on their faces, and their shoulders relaxed, as if they had been holding their breath the whole time.

Because of the invitation to contribute, the employees were excited by the definition, eager to have "EpicGreen" become part of the recruiting process, and the performance management process, and the leadership development process. They found meaning in the descriptions, rather than resentment for the people who wrote them. They were proud rather than dismissive. They bought-in to the process changes that would come as a result.

Had the leadership team of the first company invited employees to participate in the process of redefining values, they would have gotten more buy-in. Employees would have been more engaged and committed to the change the CEO was leading, and been more willing to help accelerate the transition. Instead, employees - some knowingly and some unknowingly - inhibited the process, making it harder for leaders to drive actionable change.

Yes, culture *is* hard to define. It is somewhat amorphous. But if you ask the people who live it every single day, that definition becomes much clearer, much faster.

**Out with the old:** executive leaders developing values or principles on their own and announcing them to the company.

**In with the new**: engage and involve employees in major changes to the company that they will have to live by and carry out.

**What else:** Invite input from your employees. When they are engaged in the process, they are more likely to be invested in the outcome. It's the same principle as executive coaching, consulting, and parenting: if the other person can come up with the solution on their own, they are more likely to follow through with it. On the contrary, if we tell our children the answer, they defy us. If we tell our clients the answers, they don't believe it. If we tell our employees what the values are, they will reject them, and the resentment towards senior leaders may fester. It may take a bit longer, but the outcome will always be better when people are invited to be part of the process.

# SECTION 2:
# INDIVIDUAL RELATIONSHIPS

# Annie

### The Story
I was sitting in the lobby of a Hampton Inn somewhere in the state of Maryland; it was later than I wanted it to be, given my tendency to turn into a pumpkin around 11pm, and I still had a lot of work left.  Across from me sat my colleague, her short blonde pixie cut perfectly in place.  We had been working at the same leadership consulting company for about a year and had interacted dozens of times for various reasons.  But this day marked our first true collaboration.  We were partners on a project: I designed the training content, she delivered it to the learners.

We sat there, knee deep in the work, periodically looking at our watches to know how much sleep we would have to sacrifice for this client.  Feeling a sense of unease and withdrawal, I paused in my work, momentarily gazed into nothingness, then finally looked directly at her, and asked, *"is it hard for you to work with me?"* She appeared to be a bit stunned by this question, her bright blue eyes slowly widening, but sat silently pondering the question.  Though it was merely seconds, it felt like minutes before the word *"No"* came out of her mouth. I couldn't help but feel there was a *"but"* on the way, however.

Annie is an evangelical Christian, a conservative Republican, a wife, a mother of two kids, and a Latina who lives in the San Diego suburbs in a planned community designed perfectly for the conventional family. I am basically the opposite of that. I'm white, a lesbian, an atheist, and a Democrat who has bounced between almost every major city in the Northeast Corridor (Philadelphia, New York, Boston), often living in an apartment barely larger than the bed I sleep in. I don't own a home, I don't have children, I don't have pets, and I'm not married. I knew Annie disagreed with my lifestyle, and I was certain she fiercely disagreed with my worldview, as I did hers. In fact, I feared her worldview, because as I told her, "your people don't always like my people." And frankly, I think she feared my worldview, too. What was still unknown to me at that moment, however, was how much our differences were impacting our work together.

We put our project on hold, ordered a glass of wine, sunk deeper into the Hampton Inn lobby furniture, and discussed the many nuances of our lives. For all we disagreed about, our ethics were clearly aligned on one point: we would not bill the client for this personal part of our discussion. This conversation, initiated from an invitation to explore our differences, essentially launched a social experiment that has lasted years, and has had an unbelievable, goose-bump-invoking ripple effect across parts of our country.

That night, I learned about Annie's sheltered upbringing, her conservative politics, and how her faith impacts almost every interaction and decision in her life. She heard the story of how I came out as a lesbian, learned about why I believe in liberal politics, and looked in disbelief as I described the excitement of living in New York City. We talked for hours about our differences, both in wonderment of the other. We roared with laughter as we described the way we approach intimate relationships. For her, it was traditional: she had a boyfriend, he proposed, they got married. After that, they moved in together, figured out how to live with each other, had a family, and formed a beautiful life along the way. For me? Well, I need to test drive the car before I buy it! I couldn't believe that she would get married before living with her partner and testing for compatibility. She couldn't believe I would make such a sacrilegious choice and "fornicate" (I had to research that word) with someone before marriage.

I don't think we realized it at the time, but before this conversation, there was a tenseness between us. Yes, we were doing our work, and yes I believe we were doing it well. But I could sense a barrier between us, an unspoken rift that was created by virtue of not tearing it down. Until we did. And it was amidst our laughter and surprise and storytelling and connection, that a bout of clarity came over me: **curiosity and certainty cannot coexist.**

We cannot be certain and curious at the same time, because one negates the other. When we are certain, we are closed. When we are curious, we are open. If I'm certain, I may say, "there is one God," or

"I know this is right," or "living with your partner before marriage is wrong." But if I'm curious, I may say, "I believe in one God, but what do you believe in?" or "I feel like this is right, do you have an alternative approach?" or "I could never live with my partner before marriage, what was your experience?" Questions keep us open, while statements keep us closed. Curiosity inspires us to learn, whereas certainty supposes we already know. With Annie, when I let go of certainty, stayed in the zone of curiosity, and asked her questions, the world opened up in a new way, and my appreciation for the diversity all around me - particularly in her - profoundly expanded.

The hiatus from our work that evening bridged a divide whose size was previously unknown. And it led to a better product for our client. The evening of our chat was our second of four days delivering training programs to this client, and there was a marked difference in our interactions and our delivery approach in days three and four. That improvement was due to our conversation, where we broke through the invisible tension with an invitation to learn. Sadly, Annie and I spent the first year of our working relationship ignoring - or maybe actively avoiding - our differences, putting authenticity on the backburner in favor of getting work done. I think Annie was afraid to offend me, or of getting it "wrong," while I was afraid of judgment - both my own and hers. Our different worldviews sat between us for a year before we both found the courage to learn from them. By finally addressing those differences head on, acknowledging them instead of pretending they didn't exist, and inviting the dialogue, we witnessed higher levels of productivity and even better results. Plus, we formed a lasting relationship.

Annie and I continued our ongoing engagement with each other in this courageous way. I would tell her about my dating adventures, she would tell me about the woes of raising teenagers. I would share my love and admiration for the Obamas; she would politely express her longing for a Romney (or at least a more conservative) administration. I would ask her questions about Christianity; she would ask me how I could have values instilled without a God to guide me. And that's when the next phase of our social experiment began. On a warm Spring day, from over 2000 miles away, I invited her to attend a Gay Pride Parade, and in return she invited me to attend church on Easter Sunday. We giggled with nervousness, and then proverbially shook hands through the cell towers that connected us across the country. I'll admit, I wasn't sure how serious either of us were, but merely days later, she had the parade scheduled. San Diego Pride, Summer 2016. I was impressed.

I equipped her with a first timer's guide to Pride, explaining the history of the Stonewall Riots (the impetus for the event), what she might see or experience, and just generally what to expect from her first pride parade. While I find solace and community at the parades I've gone to in the past, I can understand why she was nervous and uneasy. And I respected her even more for going, despite being slightly spooked by the whole thing. Perhaps worried that she would be judged for her conservative beliefs, or perhaps scared by the outward expressions of love that buck against the faith of the Christian church, she went anyway. While there, she chronicled her experience in a notebook like a journalist covering her beat, observing the happenings from up close and far away, seemingly at the same time.

*"Everyone was so happy,"* she exclaimed. At the parade, Annie and her husband befriended a gay man, who helped explain some of the observations from the day. When they left, Annie's husband, also a conservative Christian, shook the kind man's hand. This moment is sealed in her memory forever, and tears still show up in her eyes when she recalls the exchange between her somewhat homophobic conservative husband and a gay, HIV-positive stranger they met in the street. The imagery of the handshake is more than just symbolic; those were two people genuinely connecting, if for only a brief moment, across the greatest divide we have: fear.

A few weeks after the parade, Annie called. She sounded different. She slowly and tearfully explained to me that her sister was also a lesbian, a fact she had kept from me until this very moment.

They had only stilted conversations in the 10 years since her sister came out, and Annie's relationships with her sister's family were superficial at best. Choked up and voice shaking, she told me that because of our social experiment, she was inspired to call her sister. And after over a decade of being estranged, they had plans to reunite the next weekend. The invitation worked! And not my invitation to Annie, and not Annie's invitation to me. But the power of the invitation in general, now extended from Annie to her sister, was, quite literally, palpable.

Through the invitation to be curious, Annie realized that she could finally accept her sister's lifestyle, and to this day, they have a renewed relationship. Of course I don't know all the details of her sister's coming out story, or Annie's reactions to it, or any of the other skeletons in the family's closet. But I do know that because of our social experiment, Annie and her sister spend holidays and weekends together, their kids actually interact, and they chit chat on the phone like sisters tend to do. All this, thanks to the courage and curiosity that came to life in a Hampton Inn lobby.

Now it was my turn. Months before Easter Sunday, I got an email from Annie. She had bought me a plane ticket to fly to San Diego for Easter weekend! Despite my plan to find a public church in Philadelphia to attend, Annie was hell-bent on showing me **her** Christian church specifically, and helping me understand the ways of God through **her** eyes.  For a myriad of reasons, I felt uneasy about making the trek across the country, but in the end, this was Annie's invitation to me.  She was inviting me to be with her family, with her God, and with her community.

I got on the plane.

Annie now tells me that she was nervous for me to be there.  Not because of who I am, but because of the judgment I might bring with me.  Admittedly, I was nervous too...for the same reason - my own judgment.  But I donned my hat of curiosity, and on Good Friday, I sat in the pew trying to read along in the bible, internalize the songs, and make sense of the faith by which the people surrounding me lived their lives.  I asked a lot of questions, I tried to understand, and I tried to fit in... or at least not to stand out too much.  I learned a few things that weekend: 1) Good Friday is not good at all - it's quite solemn; 2) Saturday has a name (Holy Saturday); 3) I felt joy and love all around me on that Easter Sunday, same as Annie felt at the gay pride parade several months prior.

I left with a greater respect for the people who believe in the teachings of a God, and most importantly with empathy for how Annie lives her life, makes decisions, and determines the difference between right and wrong.  I didn't leave church a changed woman.  I did not find God, nor did I miraculously become a believer. Similarly, and unsurprisingly, Annie didn't leave the parade with a romantic interest in women. But that was never the point. We didn't set out to change each other or convince each other of anything. Our goal was only to invite a new and different life experience into our own. Our goal was to learn, and to build a connection that transcended our differences. Mission accomplished.

While visiting with Annie's family, not only did we talk about Christianity, we also couldn't help but talk about the elephant in the room: the newly elected president, Donald J. Trump. Regardless of your political persuasion, I think it's fair to say that our country's decision in November of 2016 was profound. Whether it was excitement or despair, intrigue or dread, validation or denial, the nation made a bold choice that day, and it sent us spiraling in opposite directions. But the more perspectives I invited, the more shared experiences I realized existed. A Trump-hating lesbian and a Trump-supporting young white man shared a similar brand of fear due to this election. Annie's college-aged son was afraid to wear his MAGA sweatshirt, in fear of the left-leaning students he associated with; I was afraid to show affection for my partner, in fear of the right-leaning people who felt free to express their disapproval of me. He was afraid of hate-spewing liberals, I was afraid of hate-spewing conservatives. So there we were, both essentially afraid of the other, sitting on the same couch, in the same room, in the same home. And we would never have known if not for the invitation to share our lived experiences.

It's been several years since then. There is *still* hatred coming from the evangelicals aimed at the gays, there are *still* anti-faith groups attacking Christians, and there is *still* a society riddled with animosity. Despite that, Annie and I have both continued to courageously engage in curious conversations with people different from us; still with fear, at times, but always with an invitation at the core.

**Out with the old**: avoid differences, and never talk about politics, religion, or sex.

**In with the new**: invite other people to share how they're different from you, be curious about their values and how they got them, and believe that the connections you get in the process will drive better outcomes.

**What else:** We think that avoiding differences will better serve the company. We believe that if we focus on the work, our politics or lifestyles or love interests won't get in the way. But it's actually the other way around: if we focus on our relationships, and foster humanity at work, the productivity and quality will both increase. We need to be genuinely curious about our differences, rather than pretending they don't exist. And we need to provide space in our organizations to engage in hard conversations. We need to model them. When we avoid these topics, we only broaden the divide between us. By not working to learn about others, we stay stuck in our own ways. Trying to understand our differences breeds empathy, and it is empathy that enables two people to work together, to communicate effectively, and to get more from our employees. Our cursory expression of tolerance is not enough; we need to invite people to share a piece of themselves, so we can see our differences, explore them together, learn something along the way, and build meaningful relationships at work.

## Eggshells

*TRIGGER WARNING: This gets personal. Some might say "too personal," but not me. Read on, dear reader, just be warned: this shit is heavy.*

**The Story:**
While my introduction of *invitation* as a concept was playfully presented on stage at the DisruptHR event in Philadelphia, the true inspiration occurred many, many years earlier in a more somber way. It actually started at a time in my life when I longed for an invitation to connect, when I ached for someone to invite and empathize with my experience, when I pined for a feeling of support and comfort, and when I had no deeper desire than for a meaningful relationship where I felt safe to share my story.

**This is the story that *actually* solidified the crucial need for invitation...**

A month after my 18th birthday, circa 1998, my parents brought me to the University of Delaware to start my freshman year of college. A seemingly normal and exciting experience, with one devastating exception: one of my older brothers had unexpectedly and tragically died the week prior. While camping with friends, enjoying the great outdoors, and likely enjoying a beer or two, my brother lost his life. After a long hike and an evening by the fire, he rolled himself up in his sleeping bag, unaware that he would never wake up. When his poor friends found him the next morning, any attempt at CPR was just for show, as his blue lips and stiff body were clear signs of lifelessness. He suffocated. He suffocated inside his sleeping bag. He suffocated inside his sleeping bag in the middle of the Connecticut woods, on a late summer evening.

Of course, the full family story is more complicated...

I am the youngest of three. I have, er, had, two older brothers. The week preceding his death, my parents left the country – for their first and only time – to celebrate their 25th wedding anniversary. My middle brother and I were home alone that week, while my oldest brother, then 23 years old, was in Virginia with friends. The day before my parents arrived home at Newark airport, the same night of my brother's fateful camping trip, he and I agreed that he would be home the next morning to get the car, and make the 3-hour round trip to the Northeast's most annoying airport. But that Saturday morning, the day he was being collected by a coroner, he [obviously] didn't show up at home to get the car. So I angrily and resentfully drove to New Jersey to pick up my parents. As a somewhat selfish 18-year-old, I spent the return trip complaining about my brother, rather than getting the details of their delightful tropical vacation.

Within an hour of returning home, police officers knocked on the door to share the horrific news of my brother's death. I'll never forget that moment. The sudden and intense ringing in my ears. The momentary loss of breath. The unfamiliar weakness in my legs. It was all too much to take. The six days that followed became a blurry amalgamation of grief and overwhelm, bookended by loneliness, and interspersed with familial connections.

On the seventh day after his death, however, all the fanfare came to an abrupt halt. In a somewhat robotic manner, I packed my bags, loaded the car, and pulled out of the driveway on our way to my adulthood. At the time, this just seemed normal; a pragmatic approach to a debilitatingly emotional time. Needless to say, Kevin's death made my transition to college immensely challenging, though I wish I had a more accurate word to describe it. It made all my interactions much more loaded, it stripped me of the ease and lightness one would expect on their first day of college, and it made what some would consider the biggest moment of their 18 years seem insignificant and unimportant. I wasn't even sure I should *go* to college after such a family tragedy, but we all agreed that my life shouldn't stop because my brother's life had. This was an odd revelation to have, since merely days before, while riding in the back of the death limo, my outrage and anger had coalesced into a dagger pointed at the random strangers living their lives normally. I was irate at those people who were driving to work on a

Wednesday, while I was on my way to bury my brother. *Didn't they know that the world had changed*? I felt so invisible that day, and, likely, on the day we drove to Delaware, too. My family was in such a state of shock that our already-diminished capacity for emotions was completely obliterated, and our practical side prevailed when there wasn't a clear answer to the question, "what would you do instead of college?" And since we didn't have the ability to explore how our collective emotional state might influence my life, we decided to keep moving forward as planned. In hindsight, I wish we made a different choice.

I spent the first three weeks in a fog, trying to seem normal, trying to make friends, and trying to live that carefree, exciting life that every college kid dreams about. I went to class, I got to know my roommates, I went to a frat party, I smoked pot for the first time. I faked it. I constantly vacillated between wanting to tell the story of my brother's camping trip at which he took his last breath and wanting to keep the details of his death private. I must have researched the definition of "asphyxiation" over 100 times, desperately trying to understand how he could have died in a sleeping bag. I needed support, but I didn't know how to find it. I was plagued by the common get-to-know-you question, "how many siblings do you have?" In some ways, I still am. While I worked diligently to keep the feelings at bay, they were always hanging over me. Like the sound of a refrigerator running, the dull hum of mourning was constantly present, but not always felt.

And then things got unexpectedly worse. Less than one month into my college experience, I went for a walk to get away from the seemingly immature ruckus of the dorm. I wanted to be alone and think about my brother; to grieve. It was the one-month anniversary of his death, after all. I listened to Green Day's Good Riddance (Time of Your Life) on repeat, as well as a handful of other sad songs I had available on a freshly burned CD playing on my Sony Discman. Somewhere on the walk, however, I grew suspicious, weary, and concerned. I took off my headphones, looked around in earnest, but falsely convinced myself I was being paranoid. This was the first time I had left campus; the first time I had gone for a walk alone.

Around 9:00pm on that cool September evening, a man grabbed me, put a gun in my back, dragged me into the woods, stripped me of my clothing, and raped me.

Bare on the moist forest floor, my body lay, used as an instrument for power and pleasure. My mind and spirit however, seemed to escape into the starry night sky, watching down on the evening's events. It was as if an outside force was keeping me suspended in the air, protecting me from breaking, falling, or collapsing. The pine bushes and tall grass plants stood against the old paper mill, with the overgrown weeds making it nearly impossible to see the sidewalk from which I came. The experience felt like it lasted a lifetime. In reality, it was closer to 30 minutes.

When he released me, I ran. I didn't know what direction I was running, where I was headed, or what was before me. But I ran away, never ever looking back. At some point I ran out of stamina and transitioned into walking. Soon thereafter, and with a growing concern that I was, indeed, lost, I happened upon a housing development. As luck would have it, I found a man sitting in a van outside a home. Though the statement "a man in a van outside a home" may sound creepy, this man was a good man. And without any other options obvious to me, I approached him and asked him how to get back to the University. He assured me that the only way back was in the direction from which I came. Seeing my concern about what just existed in that direction, and witnessing a somewhat-disheveled, obviously shaken woman in front of him, he kindly asked if I wanted a ride. Without another viable option, I consented. He drove me back to campus, and once I saw an area that felt familiar, I abruptly jumped out of his van. I thanked him, and sprinted back to my dorm; the place that at that time was known as "home." I don't know this man's name, I have no recollection of what he looked like, I couldn't tell you the make or model of his minivan. But he was among the most considerate people I encountered that evening.

I entered my dorm obviously shaken, and somehow within minutes the news had spread across the residence. The police were called, and I was swept away in a cruiser, barely able to catch my breath. After I left, the resident assistants had emergency meetings with every student who lived nearby. Everyone knew what happened. I was exposed, in every possible way. Literally, naked in the woods, but also through the conversations being had about me at the dorms without my approval. Several hours went by. The police were involved in an aggressive search for my missing shirt, the evidence that stained it, and the man who took it. I went to the hospital, and several hours later, around 3:00am, I was delivered back to my dorm room.

From that moment on, every path I ventured down was littered with eggshells. If I was lucky, people very delicately tried to walk on them, feeling the tender crack under their delicate feet. Many just avoided me and my eggshells all together. Not knowing what to say, the most common engagement was no engagement at all. It was likely uncomfortable for them, so they avoided me. I had a knack for silencing a room. In fact, I spent a lot of my time working to make *other* people feel better about what happened to *me*. This is the bizarre and all too common experience of many.

Let **me** make **you** feel better because **you** are uncomfortable with **my** experience.

When I was upset or emotional, my roommates, friends, and fellow dorm dwellers would remain silent, fidget in their discomfort, and look to each other to silently fight over who would speak with me. It wasn't malicious, they just had no idea how to show up, and it felt easier for everyone if we just avoided the topic altogether. They needed the silence to feel protected. *They* needed it, not me. And this was my first foray into the concept of invitation. Because every single day I yearned and silently ached for someone to show an interest in me and my story. All I wanted was someone to invite me to share what I was going through.

There were certainly people who said things like, *"if you ever want to talk..."* or *"I'm here for you if you need me..."* But it was really hard to deal with the impact of that kind of double-trauma, and I didn't have the skills at that time to appropriately ask for the help I needed. In addition to the weight of the event, I also had to manage the onus of seeking out someone who once offered to listen, admitting to them that I was upset, asking to talk, finding the right words, feeling like a burden, and not being sure they'd know what to say. That was all a bridge too far for me to cross. Instead, I politely thanked those people for their offers to listen, and stayed inside my head, where the conversations were much easier to control.

I would have given anything for a friend to find me, to initiate the conversation, and show me that they were not only "here if I needed something" but also genuinely curious and interested in my story. I didn't want to walk into a room and ruin the vibe; I didn't want to walk in and say how sad I was that my brother was dead.  But I would have loved for someone to have said *"Hey, I watched this TV show, and it made me think about what happened to you…is it hard for you to watch those shows?"* or *"I read another story in the news today; it's heartbreaking.  Did you read it?  What was your reaction?"* Or any other invitation to share.

As a friendly reminder: bringing up the trauma wouldn't have reminded me that it happened.  I assure you, I didn't forget.  Bringing up the trauma would have only made me feel less alone.  I would have really benefited from someone asking the questions, showing the interest, and taking the first step.  That way, I wouldn't have had to.  But no one did.  So, I suffered in silence.

So it was as a teenager that I learned the invaluable power of an invitation.  When someone shows up and asks you questions they genuinely want answers to…when they invite your story no matter how difficult…when they inquire about your experiences…when they show interest in the events in your life…it makes all the difference.  Game. Changer. And whether those experiences include an almost-unspeakable trauma, or just everyday living doesn't matter. It's the invitation to share them that builds the bridge to connection.

And that is what "inclusion" should feel like.

When inclusion feels like this at work, my employer gets all of my competence, all of my diligence, and all of my effort. When co-workers invite my experiences, they unlock the door to my ideas, my innovation, my problem-solving. By being curious about me, personally, they get the best of me, professionally.

**Out with the old**: if someone is going through something, it's their responsibility to ask for what they need
**In with the new:** if someone is going through something, proactively invite them to share their experiences with you

**What else:** When someone is going through something troubling, at work or personally, invite them to speak about it. Avoiding the topic under the guise of "I didn't want to upset them" is just camouflage for our own discomfort. Most of the time, if you're avoiding a difficult topic it is because it makes *you* uncomfortable, not the other person. In fact, according to a study by Bravely, 70% of employees are avoiding difficult conversations, and the humans in the workplace are suffering as a result[5]. Instead of avoidance, stay present, seek the person out, and send messages of inquiry not passivity. Don't just be there for your friends or co-workers, go out of your way to find them and ask about their progress or thoughts or feelings on the issue at hand. From big things like rape or death, to smaller things like stories of your hometown, inviting the dialogue is the key to creating an inviting workplace. As was the case with me, this approach can literally save someone's life.

*Side Bar:* *If not for the almost-unspeakable trauma I endured as a teenager, I wouldn't be where I am today as an adult. And while I would have loved to learn my life lessons another way, that just wasn't my path. Odd as it might be (and feel) to admit: I'm grateful for all I've experienced, because I am healthier, more authentic, and more grounded because of it. In the end (well, in the middle, really - I still have a long way to go!), life is good. :-)*

---

[5] https://learn.workbravely.com/hubfs/Understanding-the-Conversation-Gap.pdf?t=1533596048056&utm_campaign=smart%20brief%20test&utm_source=hs_automation&utm_medium=email&utm_content=64321921&_hsenc=p2ANqtz-4k_KzRnQlCrerxB5Gr0XEMMWshlLmigMT3ElhTx6htsOUK3kcp7H-J_GAqZMvIAdILhbkkDX2sEDVSXIQdx9e-xqh8A&_hsmi=64321921

# SECTION 3:
# TEAM RELATIONSHIPS

## Letting Go

**The Story:**
I was working at a start-up company in lower Manhattan. I had been there almost three years when seemingly out of the blue, I had a meeting with one of the owners who said that he would be lowering my salary and taking away some of my responsibilities. There wasn't much explanation, despite a cursory statement about expectations.

My role at this company was to manage our corporate events. From venue selection to logistics to vendor management to guest services, I managed it all. Along the way, I found a few vendors who not only gave us fair deals, but they also stuck with us for every event (regardless of location) and were more than happy to go beyond the scope of their roles to help us. These vendors knew our business and could predict what we needed before we needed it, making our interactions seamless. They became part of our extended family, helping us succeed at every turn. They were not merely vendors providing value, they were partners.

The owner of the company I worked for felt that I was purposely using vendors that were *not* the cheapest possible, thereby not prioritizing the company's best interests (i.e., profit). The bottom line was simple: we had different versions of what "best interests" were. I was happy to pay a bit more for ease and confidence and trust; he wanted the highest profit possible, with no regard to the quality of the company's events. Either way, we were at odds, and things did not improve in the following weeks.

In fact, things ended with me claiming I would call my family's lawyer (sidebar: my dad was a gym teacher; we didn't have a family lawyer), and that triggered my boss to immediately shut down all of my computer and email access in response. Suffice to say, I had been fired, without the formality of a conversation. In hindsight, this actually worked in my favor, as I was going to graduate school three months later, and this afforded me a bit of a poor woman's sabbatical. But inside, I was devastated. This was the only time to date that I had been fired. I felt like a failure, I felt betrayed, and I was ashamed.

Looking back, what I wish he would have done was invited me to leave. Actually, I wish he would have invited a conversation about the values under which I was operating, and how they aligned or were misaligned with the company's values. But, I would have settled for a conversation where we honestly and candidly said that things weren't working. And rather than just demoting me and ultimately shutting down my access, I wish he would have invited me to resign. Sure, there would need to be some form of financial agreement, but I'd argue that a severance is a less expensive way to go than to drag out a demotion, justify a pay reduction, initiate performance improvement plans, and engage in mutually frustrating conversations. This is not to say that every employee having performance struggles should be fired. On the contrary, we should help employees to perform at their best as much as we can. But we've all been privy to the moments when it becomes clear that things will just not work. And in those moments, our tendency to drag out the process becomes painful for everyone involved. I think we're better served offering an invitation to exit the company with integrity and dignity.

If this sounds like a radical idea, let me remind you of the legend Patty McCord, the former Chief People Officer at Netflix and author of the book "Powerful." She argues that instead of putting people on a 90-day Performance Improvement Plan, having laborious conversations about it throughout that 90-day period, and ultimately letting them go…we should just be candid that it's not working, and pay them a three-month severance. Inviting someone to leave is a kinder, more direct way of managing performance.

About 10 years after I had been fired, I was managing a team that consisted of eight learning and development employees. I had one employee who was struggling. She was struggling with her performance, she was struggling to be engaged with her work, she was struggling to come to work without crying! In one conversation, I simply - and empathetically - asked, *"what is the point?"* I was genuinely curious. *"What is the point of coming to work if you're crying on your way in, you're *miserable, and you're not contributing at the level you'd like?"* This was met with silence. I then invited her to take a week off from work. It wasn't a punishment - I didn't take away her vacation days or any of her salary. She just needed a break to rest and regroup.

One week later, she returned. We met again, and together devised a plan that enabled her to leave the company in six months. This left her time to figure out what she really wanted to do, and to search for what was next. It also left me time to find her replacement, and it allowed me to help her transition out of the organization. To be clear: there were strict performance and engagement expectations that she had to meet, and in return I would help guide her to her next career move. It was a win-win, and an example of what the NeuroLeadership Institute calls "optimal inclusion:" making sure people feel included in the right ways at the right time without compromising speed of execution[6]. In this case, the company got six months of knowledge transfer, and an employee who was "all-in" and committed to doing a great job. Additionally, the employee got the support and loyalty she deserved after more than 10 years at the company, parting with respect and appreciation for the organization.

---

[6] https://neuroleadership.com/your-brain-at-work/optimal-inclusion-creates-better-teams

What was my invitation to her? It was an invitation to leave, to quit, to find a better fit. I didn't fire her, and it wasn't a contentious argument. We had a mature, thoughtful, empathetic, and candid conversation about the state of things, and we both agreed that it wasn't working. Something needed to change. And it did.

**Out with the old:** long, drawn out exit conversations, often controlled by Legal or HR, inspired by avoiding backlash.

**In with the new**: respectful, mature conversations that highlight what isn't working, and the option to fix it or transition out.

**What else:** Empower and upskill managers to have dignified conversations. There will always be times when we have to face the reality that it's not working with a particular employee. Have the dignity to call it out, engage in a thoughtful conversation, and invite the person to resign (or change jobs, or something else). Put the employee's best interests first: if they are unhappy in the job, and nothing has worked to change that, then help them find a job that's a better fit! They will reward you with loyalty and cooperation, rather than disengagement and legal retaliation. Update your HR policies and practices in this regard and stop letting the legal threshold dictate our humanity.

## Feedback As a Gift

**The Story:**
*"Would you come to the course I'm facilitating, and then let me know how I can be more effective?"*

This was the simple, yet profound question Alison asked me. She was fairly new to the role of learning program facilitator, and wanted help honing her craft. As you can imagine, the answer to her question was an absolute, unabashed, enthusiastic "YES!" Being invited to provide feedback like this is any manager's dream. But Alison's invitation to me wasn't quite as straightforward as it may have seemed. The result of her invitation had significant meaning, to me, her, and the organization.

When she invited me to give her feedback, I felt seen for my expertise. She wasn't just asking me because I was her manager; she was asking me for my experience and my competence in the area of facilitation. I felt good about myself, confident in what I had to offer, and even more elated at the opportunity to share that knowledge. When I showed up to observe her, I was 100% tuned in. There was no laptop open, no phone on the desk, no distractions. I was fully present and paid attention to everything she did and said, so I could give her useful and detailed feedback, for which she had asked. This is something employees likely want from their manager: someone who is 100% present and eager to help them. Most employees likely want a manager they trust to give them useful feedback, to help them get better at whatever they are doing, and to engage in meaningful work together.

**In the employee's eyes, it is not "give me feedback," it's "help me grow."**

Despite the desire for that level of devotion from our managers, so many are distracted by emails, trying to comply with an unspoken, unrealistic expectation of response time. So many managers are caught up in the frantic day-to-day lifestyle of meetings and emails, that they neglect their responsibility to give attention to the employees who want to grow and develop in their career.

But in the case of Alison, because I was invited to be there, it didn't feel like an obligation or a responsibility. In that scenario, I knew I was wanted in the room, and I knew I could help her. When I was giving her feedback, not only was I feeling grateful and humbled and respected, I was also able to provide meaningful, relevant observations with examples and suggestions for improvement! To this day, Alison and I (we no longer work together) have a great relationship, with this experience at the heart.

Additionally, when Alison invited me to give her feedback, she unknowingly changed her mindset and disposition. She was automatically open to critiques of her performance, she was eager to be more effective, and therefore not defensive at all. She had asked for the feedback, so emotionally and mentally, she was ready for it. She wanted it. It changed the entire feedback giver/receiver relationship. Not only did she *hear* the feedback, she internalized it, clarified it, and even practiced some of the suggestions for improvement right then and there. Two weeks later, I observed her again, and there was noticeable improvement in her performance.

In preparing this story, I asked Alison to reflect on that interaction to make sure I wasn't blowing it out of proportion. Her response: "that was easily the most impactful hour I've had in the last six months."

According to Forbes, 65% of employees say they want more feedback. Yet managers tend to think of giving feedback as a chore, a responsibility, or the fulfilling of a duty, rather than responding to a request. I posit that there is a fear that the receiver will be defensive, reactive, or emotional, and this discomfort is easier to avoid than confront. Which explains why "providing feedback" is among the most common topics of corporate training. But despite the popularity of this training and the apparent need for the topic, only 14.5% of managers strongly agree that they are effective at providing feedback.

Rather than recommend the same solution to the same problem hoping for a different result, why not reject that insanity and try something new? Rather than teach managers to give feedback, like we've been doing unsuccessfully for decades, why not teach everyone to *ask* for it? So often, we put the onus on managers to provide feedback, but if the relationship is flipped, and the employee invites that feedback, the feedback becomes responsive, not forceful. It becomes an offering, not a requirement.

So many times, we have heard that "feedback is a gift," yet in the book *Thanks for The Feedback,* they say it's more like getting a colonoscopy! Maybe that is because - like with a colonoscopy - the receiver hasn't asked for it, they haven't invited it, and they aren't emotionally ready to hear it. On the contrary, when employees really want to improve their performance, and ask their manager how, they'll get more meaningful and comfortable information. And in turn, managers will be gifted with grateful employees like Alison. And the manager/employee relationship becomes more and more significant, which only increases the shared feedback down the line.

**Out with the old**: training leaders and managers to *give* feedback

**In with the new:** training all employees, including managers and leaders, to *invite* feedback

**What else:** Change the feedback paradigm to be about inviting rather than receiving. Flip the training approach on its head, and train employees to ask their managers for feedback on their performance, or on their behavior. By being curious and invitational, we can have our employees asking questions like Alison did, and (most of) their managers will be honored to receive such a request. When we use models like the "start, stop, continue" method, or ask the "how can I be more effective?" question, we are likely receiving responses like "can't think of anything" or "I guess it's OK." That may occur because such a broad question can yield intimidation and paralysis rather than candor and openness. The standard, often-robotic, formulaic approaches to these conversations don't work. Most employees - regardless of level - want to be more effective. Let's teach them how to ask for the input that will get them there. And then we can hire for the very values of wanting continuous improvement (which leads to the behavior of inviting feedback).

## Any Questions?

**The Story:**
I was at the company's offsite retreat for the senior leadership team. We had hired a new CEO about six months prior, the company was going through major organizational change, and this was an opportunity to bring the most senior leaders together to catalyze the next steps in the company's journey.

The CEO started the two-day meeting. He spoke for about two hours, sharing information about strategy, the industry, the company's successes, and the areas of focus. At the end of his presentation, he asked the audience of more than 100 of the top leaders in the company, "*does anyone have any questions?*" Silence. "*Does this make sense to people?*" Silence. "*Any questions at all?*" Silence. Hearing nothing, the CEO carried on to the next session.

Despite the lack of questions, the rumblings at the tables told a different story. There was confusion, concerns, and an overall disengagement with the CEO's presentation. The dialogue amongst the audience contained complaints and grievances, leading to an active dissent from the CEO's message. The audience was the top 100 leaders in the 5000-person company. This was a group of smart, driven, talented people. They came to the retreat ready to engage, to offer their expertise, to explore challenging topics, and - of course - to ask questions! And we would want them to have questions, because their questions would force *everyone* to think deeper, and give us the opportunity to deliver something even better. But there was silence when the question was asked. Why?

With an audience of this size, if the speaker asks, "any questions?" one of two things will happen. Either a) there will be silence, which will be awkward for everyone, particularly the speaker; or b) the speaker will entertain questions from only the most extroverted, outgoing, gregarious employees, limiting the viewpoints heard in the room. In our case, we got option A, though the risk for option B is just as great. Both options leave a significant part of the population out of the conversation. We either miss the audience interaction altogether, as was the case with the CEO, or we will miss voices from people who are *not* members of the privileged faction of society or extroverted, outgoing employees. When we open the conversation to a large group, typically the first, and often the only people who engage are those with authority. That usually includes men, white people, and extroverts, and leaves out women, people of color, introverts, people from countries with higher power distance, and others who lack the safety or comfort in speaking out in this way.

I recommend deploying a third (or fourth or fifth) option to bring more voices into the conversation. The more voices we hear, the higher the likelihood that our outcome will be better. And in the case of a senior leadership meeting, inviting more voices to the dialogue will increase commitment to the strategy, highlight risks or dependencies before employees further down in the management chain begin acting on the strategy, increase alignment across the company, and build relationships among those leading the organization.

Critics of this approach may argue that we don't have time to include so many voices in the conversation. They are correct in asserting that a more invitational approach does require more time up front. But it saves time and wasted resources down the road. You either make time now for alignment and commitment, or you will spend time later fixing misalignment and convincing people to get on board with the company direction. Either way is time spent.

**Out with the old**: the presenter gives his/her presentation and then asks if there are any questions at the end, and when there is silence assumes the answer is "no."

**In with the new:** the presenter invites questions and interactions before, after and during presentations in a way that allows more voices to be heard.

**What else:** Change your mindset from "presentation" to "engagement." Certainly, part of engaging an audience requires a stellar presentation. And, if your goal is engagement, you can do even more to your presentation to bring the audience along with you. If there is time, use varying methods (surveys, etc.) to solicit questions prior to the event, and then incorporate the answers to those questions in the presentation itself. Doing so demonstrates that you care what is on their minds and that you listen to what they have to say. You can also engage during the presentation itself by using polling software, real-time surveys, or even sticky notes at tables to get people to submit their questions in real time! Invite them to talk to a neighbor, discuss a topic at their tables, or submit questions anonymously. Doing so sends the message that you want to hear from people, and you want to answer their questions. Simply asking "any questions?" is not an effective way to engage and doesn't make the audience feel truly invited to the dialogue. In fact, it seems like an obligatory question that anyone on the stage must ask, and will yield suboptimal interaction, at best.

## The Perimeter

**The Stor(ies):** *(in this section there are three stories, all depicting a nuanced way to use invitation at work to drive better results)*

(A)
Carly is one of three women on a support team inside a large consulting company. While she has the gift of being outspoken and sufficiently confident, she is also acutely aware of being the only woman in most of the meetings of which she is part. Often, she feels as though she needs to adjust her style to fit in. This is not an uncommon experience for those who are not part of the majority. Often, the marginalized members of our teams feel the need to assimilate and to fit in. And all too often, this tendency leads to those in the minority silencing their voices.

Tim, Carly's boss, knows this dynamic exists inside of groups and teams. He goes out of his way to ask for Carly's perspective. "If you think I'm wrong, please challenge me," he often says. This type of invitation is just what Carly needs to feel a bit more authorized to voice her opinion. Even though her opinion might not be the same as Tim's, and even if her opinion doesn't align with her mostly male team members, by being invited into the conversation, Carly can feel safe to disagree or challenge the decision. By asking her to challenge his thinking, he is inviting the dialogue, he is inviting the professional battle of ideas, and he is looking for the best approach, knowing that he needs the diversity of perspectives to come up with the best solutions.

----

(B)
The night before my first day in my new position, I flew to the Netherlands. For the record, a red-eye flight through the night into a foreign country with brand new coworkers is not my preferred way to start at a new company. No one looks cute on an overnight flight. No one. But alas, there I was.

Briana, my new teammate, was leading a two-day brainstorm session so our team could develop the initiatives and goals for the upcoming year. The group included five American colleagues, four Dutch colleagues, and two British colleagues. About halfway through the first day, someone made an observation that the people doing most of the speaking were the Americans and the British, making the Dutch folks seem rather quiet, by comparison.

Despite being in their country, we were conducting business in English. And since English was their second language, most of them needed a little time to translate all the thoughts and ideas being shared in the room. Since their cultural norms encourage slightly more subdued behavior (compared to Americans), it was difficult for them to find their voices in a way that felt authentic and appropriate.

Picking up on this dynamic, Briana adjusted the meeting. She politely, and skillfully, invited some voices to stay quiet, and then overtly invited her Dutch colleagues' opinions. She also split the larger team into three smaller groups, ensuring the groups included folks from all the regions. In this way, Briana was able to provide the right environment for *everyone* to participate to their fullest, and deliberately set up a way to invite *all* voices to be heard.

----

(C)
As part of my role in my new company, I was expected to lead internal communications, globally. I took an inventory of what we had communicated prior to me starting. I came across a document that was well-designed, easy to read, and had a little flair (which is not always the case with Human Resources information).

Referring to one of the corporate values, this document had "Killing It!" on one side of the paper, with examples of what living the values *well* would look like. On the other side of the paper, it read "Killing Us!" and listed examples of what it would look like to live the values *poorly* (or not at all). At first glance, I liked it, and I was excited to use this informal yet effective approach moving forward.

However, the terms "killing it" and "killing us," while understood broadly across America, are not appropriately translated into other languages. In fact, a literal translation could leave someone quite perplexed or even frightened, wondering why we were writing in such violent terms. Clearly, no one, including me, had thought to invite the perspective and advice from our international colleagues. Call this an oversight, call this hegemony, call this ignorance. But don't call it inclusion.

----

These are all relevant examples of how the invitation can and should be used. In all these stories, the key to success is the person or people in the majority finding the people who were sitting on or near the perimeter and inviting them to participate. The perimeter could include introverts, people of color, people whose first language is not what is being spoken, and the otherwise quiet voices (figuratively or literally). So often in our workplaces, we expect everyone to express their voices equally, without truly acknowledging the invisible barriers that exist for some, but not for all. If we expect everyone to have an equal voice, we will undoubtedly miss out on some exceptional peoples' input. We must invite the voices we want to hear from, and it is incumbent on those of us in, and with, power to make the invitation; not the other way around.

**Out with the old:** Assume and expect that if people have something to contribute, they will.

**In with the new:** Inviting people on or close to the perimeter to contribute more fully

**What else:** If you're a man, proactively seek the opinions and ideas of the women on your team. If you're a white person, proactively seek the opinions and thoughts of the people of color on your team. If you're straight, find the gays; if you're in the office, find a remote employee; if you're based in the U.S., find someone in another country; if English is your first language, find someone whose first language is something else; if you're in marketing, find a developer; if you're the extrovert, find the quiet one. And on and on and on… Accept the power you have as an invitation to create a more inclusive environment. Use your position in the company and in society to invite those on the perimeter to share their ideas, to challenge yours, to give you advice, and to overall contribute more fully.

# SECTION 4:
# INVITING DIVERSITY

## Value Connection Over Perfection

In this country, we are all part of a paradigm in which power and authority sit with one type of profile, and while we continuously work to shift it, there is an undercurrent that perpetuates the status quo. When the explicit became threatened, it shifted to become implicit, going underground to ensure its survival. What was once an obvious sign banning Black people from participation is now subversive and subtle behavior coupled with coded language that dissuades that Black person from joining altogether. Sure, it may be harder to prove in court, but it has the same negative impact and prohibits us from making more progress.

To be clear, this is not a D&I book, nor does it include all the answers to the deeply rooted systemic problems we face in the United States. The problems are powerful and far-reaching, and if I had the answers to them, not only would I be shouting them from the rooftops, I'd likely only have those answers because someone else found them, long before I got to the fight. No, I don't have a solution to these latent issues, but I do have a suggestion. The same suggestion that I touted from a stage in Philadelphia at a local DisruptHR event: *invitation*.

I believe that invitation is **one step** in the right direction.

I think it's important to acknowledge that we are all part of an interwoven series of systems. The social systems, the governmental systems, the educational systems, the legal systems, the corporate systems...they are all interconnected.

> As Martin Luther King Jr. said, "...*all mankind is tied together; all life is interrelated, and we are all caught in an inescapable network of mutuality, tied in a single garment of identity. Whatever affects one directly, affects all indirectly.*"

Dr. King is referring to all the systems of which we are members. These systems provide power and status to some, and not to others. These systems place White people superior to Blacks, Straight people higher up than Gays, men above women. And as someone within that hierarchy, it is my responsibility to use the power given to me to make change for good. Given this country's history, we know that these systems in which we all operate were created on a bedrock of racism (and many other -isms). But the willing within those systems can offer invitations that have the potential to challenge the entire architecture. This concept mirrors our society. If women could have given themselves the right to vote, I'm confident they would have done so earlier. If Black people could have written the 14th Amendment, it's likely they would have penned it long before 1868. If gay people could have made marriage legal for themselves, we would have been married for decades longer than we are now. The list goes on. The people in the *majority* granted these rights to the people being marginalized, and that same power structure exists in our companies. So if we all embrace the spirit of invitation, we can systematically change the systems. Let's invite people different from us to join the organization, and to come to the event, and to partake in the training, and to contribute to the meeting...and so on, and so on, and so on. Let's invite the stories of others, let's invite feedback from people with less status, let's invite the quiet ones to share their opinions. Let's use our power and privilege to open the space for more people who are not like us.

In my experience, I have found that most people are on board with the concept of being inclusive but struggle with knowing what to do. And if you're reading this book, it's likely safe to say that you, too, are in favor of shifting the paradigm. But how?

**People are scared to do or say the *wrong* thing, they can't identify the *right* thing, so they do *nothing*, which is often the *worst* thing.**

This tendency, caused by fear, produces a proverbial stutter. And, in some cases, a literal stutter. We start and stop, we backtrack, we fidget, we are visibly uncomfortable. We use more words than necessary. We fiercely defend our intentions. We use minimizing language like "just" and "uh" and "but" and "ah" and "maybe." And the people to whom we're speaking are left with a perpetual eye roll, as they wait patiently for their turn to join the conversation. The hesitance in our voice shows in our body, we stumble on our words, and the interaction is, at best, awkward and off putting.

Just for a minute, imagine a funeral; we've all been to one. Someone dies, and we don't know what to say to the loved ones left behind. We don't want to upset them, we don't want to say the wrong thing, we don't know how to make them feel better, so we typically say nothing, or maybe just hide behind the safety of the requisite "I'm sorry," and hope for the best. Sadly, this awkward little dance leaves no one feeling more connected, more safe, or more comforted during the hardship. The opportunity to deepen the relationship passes, and we find the fastest route back to our comfort zone, often plagued with regret.

While it may be an odd comparison, the dance at the funeral is like the conversation we have about diversity. And the impact of this waltz in the world of work is that we enact behaviors of passivity and claim them to be inclusive. Employees tend to think that by virtue of **not** being **ex**clusive, they are automatically **in**clusive. But that's not the way it works. If you are not intentionally including people, you are unintentionally excluding them.

**If you are not intentionally including people, you are unintentionally excluding them.**

The way to intentionally include someone is to invite them.  Invite them to share their ideas, their perspectives, their experiences, their opinions, their stories.  Invite them to sit at your table – literally and figuratively.  Invite them to join you, join your team, join your company.  Invite them to ask questions, invite them to give you feedback, invite them to disagree with you, invite them to challenge the way you do things.  Like Jenny on the bus, invite that person to sit down next to you (in the sweetest voice Forrest had ever heard).

In a world plagued by variant expressions of -isms, the pressure to "get it right," while woefully misplaced, can be daunting at best, and paralyzing at worst.  But therein lies the problem.  If you delay a conversation with someone different from you in hopes that you will consistently "get it right," you will miss a myriad of moments, and the opportunity for connection will sadly pass you by.  Being willing to have the conversation means being willing to mess it up.  And being willing to mess up means being willing to own it, to learn from it, and to try it again.  As Maya Angelou once said, "Do the best you can until you know better.  Then when you know better, do better."

That marriage between the courage to have the conversation and vulnerability to admit your mistake is what creates connection. Saying something with good intent, totally fucking it up, owning the impact it had and getting better IS how we deepen our relationships. The relationships we have where we never make mistakes are not true relationships – they're interviews. Relationships aren't derived from saying everything right, they are cultivated through curiosity and a genuine interest in someone else's experience. And when you have curiosity and interest, you invite someone to share more of themselves. It's almost as simple as that.

But I would be remiss if I did not highlight what I feel is obvious but may escape the conscious thought of some. For those of us in the majority, the intent of the invitation is to broaden and deepen our relationships. It is NOT because people of color require the pity of White folks. It is not because gay people are weak. It is not because women need men. It is not to prove anything to investors or voters or supporters. It is not an excuse to spout "thank you for your service." It is not a means to an end. It is not solely to increase diversity to achieve some status, public or otherwise, nor is it a prop to show on social media. The invitation is not meant to tokenize or highlight difference. It is not intended to meet a quota, a target, or a goal.

It is just one way to engage with people different from you. And for those of us in the minority: sure, it feels good to be invited, but that is *not* a prerequisite to showing up.

~~~~~~~~~~~~~~~~~~~

I'd love to live in a world where the power structures were more equitable. I am fighting for that world. I'm donating to that world. But that world is still a dream. People are judged by the content of the character only *after* they are judged by the color of their skin. So people who look like me continue to have more privilege than people who look like Dr. King. Having privilege doesn't mean I haven't worked hard, it doesn't mean I'm not smart, it doesn't mean I haven't struggled. It just means that the color of my skin (or gender or size or age, etc.) never held me back. And with that privilege, it is my responsibility to open more doors, and share more opportunities with people who haven't historically had the luxuries that I have. And I do that through an invitation.

The invitation is fundamental to hearing more, and different voices. If we simply wait for people to step up on their own, we will continue to hear from the same voices. We will rely on the extroverted, authorized, empowered individual who feels they can speak their mind freely without consequence or fear of being shunned (a privilege marginalized people rarely get). The nondominant voices - the ones we claim we want to hear - will remain silent. So, an "open door policy" isn't enough. An "if you want to talk..." isn't enough. Saying the word "meritocracy" isn't enough. If we don't invite our employees to share their opinions, provide their perspectives, and offer their ideas, we will likely lose out on the value that lives within those voices.

**If you don't look like me, you probably don't think like me. And if you don't think like me, you can help me think differently.**

Hearing new and different ideas is how we innovate. Hearing different experiences is how we break into new markets. Hearing new perspectives is how we expand the ways in which our customers rely on us. The list of benefits goes on and on. And those benefits are only realized when we build a truly inclusive company.

Today, we see major US corporations marching in the gay pride parades, we see executive-level support in the form of a "Chief Diversity Officer," we see billions of dollars invested in corporate training, and we see lots of socio-political activism shedding light on the pay gap between men and women, noting that for women of color the gap is even larger. And while the public outcry is helping to spark overdue conversations, what truly makes an organization inclusive is not how much money they spend on training, the size of the banner at the Pride Parade, the black background on their social media feed, or how many people with orange hair they showcase on their website.

What makes an inclusive company is knowing that Black and Brown people are on the leadership team; that gay people are at the table when decisions are being made; that women are on the Board; that our external marketing profiles nontraditional families; that suppliers are made up of minority-owned businesses; that investors are in all age groups; the list goes on.  What makes a company inclusive is knowing that it is safe to be me, and that I have the same opportunity to succeed as the person sitting next to me.  And the only way I know that to be true is by the relationships I build within the company. An inclusive culture is built on relationships, and the foundation to an inclusive relationship rests with an invitation.

If we want to change the existing system of which we are all a part, we must change our approach. With a culture of invitation, we will build more meaningful relationships, we will bring humanity back to the workplace, and we will ultimately create a workplace that works for everyone - not just those who have learned how to navigate the archaic unwritten rules of the road.

**A culture of *inclusion* may open the doors for everyone...but a culture of *invitation* asks them to come inside.**

## SOURCES CITED ALONG THE WAY:

https://hbr.org/2018/11/9-out-of-10-people-are-willing-to-earn-less-money-to-do-more-meaningful-work

https://www.shrm.org/hr-today/news/all-things-work/pages/the-search-for-meaning.aspx

https://www.betterup.com/en-us/about-us/news-and-press/workers-value-meaning-at-work-new-research-from-betterup-shows-just-how-much-theyre-willing-to-pay-for-it

https://hbr.org/2015/09/how-to-build-the-social-ties-you-need-at-work

https://www.gallup.com/workplace/267251/why-employees-fed-feedback.aspx

https://www.forbes.com/sites/victorlipman/2016/08/08/65-of-employees-want-more-feedback-so-why-dont-they-get-it/?sh=412d63f6914a

https://trainingindustry.com/wiki/leadership/the-leadership-training-market/

https://kids.frontiersin.org/article/10.3389/frym.2017.00046

https://headheartbrain.com/resources/how-an-understanding-of-neuroscience-can-help-create-inclusion/

https://www.psychologytoday.com/us/blog/between-cultures/201704/belonging

http://shapiroconsulting.co.uk/wp-content/uploads/2013/09/Inclusive-Leadership-Executive-Summary.pdf

https://learn.workbravely.com/hubfs/Understanding-the-Conversation-Gap.pdf?t=1533596048056&utm_campaign=smart%20brief%20test&utm_source=hs_automation&utm_medium=email&utm_content=64321921&_hsenc=p2ANqtz-_4k_KzRnQlCrerxB5Gr0XEMMWshlLmigMT3ElhTx6htsOUK3kcp7H-J_GAqZMvIAdILhbkkDX2sEDVSXIQdx9e-xqh8A&_hsmi=64321921

https://neuroleadership.com/your-brain-at-work/optimal-inclusion-creates-better-teams

*Thanks for the Feedback: The Science and Art of Receiving Feedback Well* by Douglas Stone & Sheila Heen

*Emotional Agility: Get Unstuck, Embrace Change, and Thrive in Work and Life* by Susan David

www.ingramcontent.com/pod-product-compliance
Lightning Source LLC
Chambersburg PA
CBHW050246220526
45465CB00002B/571